# The 492$^{nd}$ and the 491$^{st}$ B Norfolk

## Who were the 492$^{nd}$ and 491$^{st}$ & why Norfolk?

The 492$^{nd}$ and 491$^{st}$ Bombardment Groups were a part of the Second Air Division of the USAAF, which was itself a part of the USAAF Eighth Air Force.

During the turbulent days of World War II, Norfolk and the wider East Anglia became home to the American Mighty Eighth Air Force as it took advantage of the relatively short flight time between the Norfolk coast and the European mainland to get its war planes to Germany, occupied France and back, in the most advantageous manner. North Pickenham was one of the last of the Norfolk airfields to be completed and become operational. Its occupants had a turbulent war.

In the early part of its existence North Pickenham became home to the 492$^{Nd}$ BG. Made up of the 856$^{th}$, 857$^{th}$, 858$^{th}$ and 859$^{th}$ Bombardment Squadrons. At its height Station 143, as North Pickenham was known to the American military, was the home to almost 2,900 men and women who flew and maintained the B24 Liberators of the 492$^{nd}$ and later the 491$^{st}$ that operated on an almost daily basis into the German heartland and to the allied ground forces front line. After a mere 89 days and 67 missions the 492$^{nd}$ were decimated, losing almost half its aircrew KIA, missing or POW. They certainly gave as good as they got, but the losses could not continue. So the 491$^{st,}$ who desperately needed a new home after the catastrophic destruction of the bomb dump at their previous base, Station 366 Metfield, then took up the mantle and continued with the 852$^{nd}$, 853$^{rd}$, 854$^{th}$ and 855$^{th}$ Bombardment Squadrons taking the war to Hitler's now dwindling empire.

This is how it looked to them, recorded on a day to day basis in photographs taken by their own cameras, and on some rare stills pulled from an early colour movie film.

North Pickenham Aerodrome (Station 143) taken in December 1944.

The longest runway is North-East / South-West (06/240 – 1900 yards). Unusually for an A Class airfield it has all the hard stands to the north and west of the main runway with the accommodation and administrive sites orientated south and east. They can be seen to the lower centre and mid upper right of the photo.
The railway line crossing the photo in the top right hand corner was the LNER line linking King's Lynn to East Dereham. The local station was Holme Hale about a mile to the east.

The market town of Swaffham was just two and a half miles to the north-west and the larger conurbation of the port of King's Lynn a further twelve miles in the same direction.

Post war the airfield became the home to an RAF Thor guided missile site until eventually closing in the early sixties. It then went back to agriculture and the international Norfolk turkey industry; with one of the regions premier Kart racing tracks locating in the south-west corner of the site. A Radio transmitter mast is also located on the southern edge of the site and is a notable visual identifying point for local pilots.

A small selection of memorabilia and photos are still to be seen in the Blue Lion Pub in the centre of the village; a pub frequented by the men of the $492^{nd}$ and $491^{st}$ during their stay in Norfolk.

# The 492nd Bombardment Group.

The 492$^{nd}$ were the first operational bomb group to take up residence at North Pickenham. However their story starts long before then and can be traced back to the 104$^{th}$ Observation Squadron of the Maryland National Guard in Baltimore. As the bomb group that eventually arrived in East Anglia, it was late '43 to early '44 that saw the formation of the 492$^{nd}$ solidify into a heavy bomb group.
From the 11$^{th}$ of May to the 7$^{th}$ of August they flew 67 operational missions over Nazi occupied Europe.

They had flown over to England without the loss of a single plane, but their luck would not hold out much longer and they started to lose men and machines at a rate that became unsustainable. Despite all these losses, they never failed to make the target, nor did they scatter and disperse in the face of the devastating firepower put up by German ack-ack guns, or the fighters of the Luftwaffe.

Nevertheless the high command wanted changes and as the 492$^{nd}$'s losses were unacceptable for any bomb group, however brave, they were disbanded and dispersed in August '44.

The losses for the USAAF were 1.6%; the 492$^{nd}$'s were running at 44.2%.

---

The first mission brought the first crash and the first fatality…
     …for the 492$^{nd}$ it was just the beginning, there would be no happy ending.

Despite the tremendous losses, the B24s of the 492$^{nd}$ left the safety of Norfolk, on an almost daily basis and headed out over Europe to hit back hard at the enemy's war machine…

And while the aircrews were the undoubted heroes of the squadrons, the ground crews were their backbone, from readying a new engine to be fitted to one of the B24s …

…to simply pulling the planes around to get them in the right place.

From replacing damaged skin panels…

…to working the wrecker wagon…

…or packing those all important parachutes; whatever the job, the boys on the ground supported their air crews all the way.

They were also usually responsible for the nose art that
had an essential place on all USAAF bomber stations…

…North Pickenham was no exception.

Some were very traditional…

…others were plain and simple. But just look at the impressive row of mission indicators.

…As with all stations, glamour and humour…

…shared top billing on a B24's nose.

Some were very obvious…

…others you had to be there to fully understand.

Then some needed a serious paint restoration when they were transferred in from other 2$^{nd}$ Air Division stations. El Capitan came (well used) from the 44$^{th}$ Bomb Group at Shipdham.

Other new arrivals just 'dropped in' like this. A P38 Lightning that then managed to trip over at the end of the runway.

On July 20th 1944, this B17G arrived unexpectedly, then shed a landing wheel in the process.

This Mosquito copied the B17, just five days later but managed to shed both sets of main gear and its starboard prop as well.

Having caught fire in mid-air, this Vaultee Vengeance had nowhere to go but down…
…fortunately Nth Pickenham was within range.

Accidents and crashes were not only seen and recorded by the USAAF. This unique photo sequence of the wreckage of the Arnett crew's B24 'Boomerang' brought down over enemy held Holland, was taken by the first German soldiers on the scene. (Later stolen by a member of the Dutch resistance.)

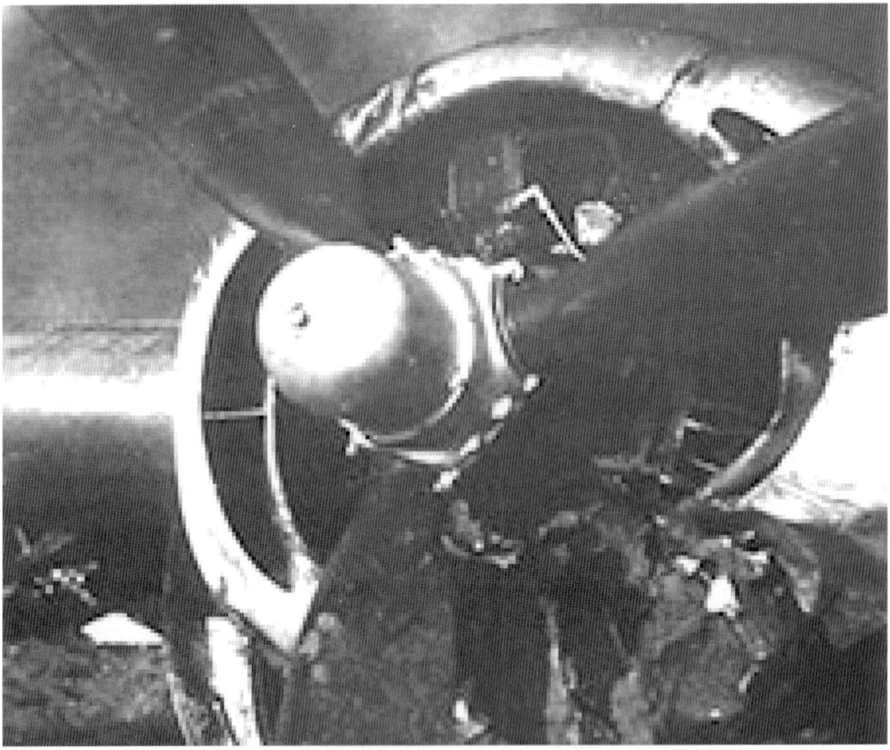

A close up of a prop and engine taken by a German soldier…

…or a shot of his chums standing by the wreckage; similar in a lot of ways to the photos taken back at North Pickenham.

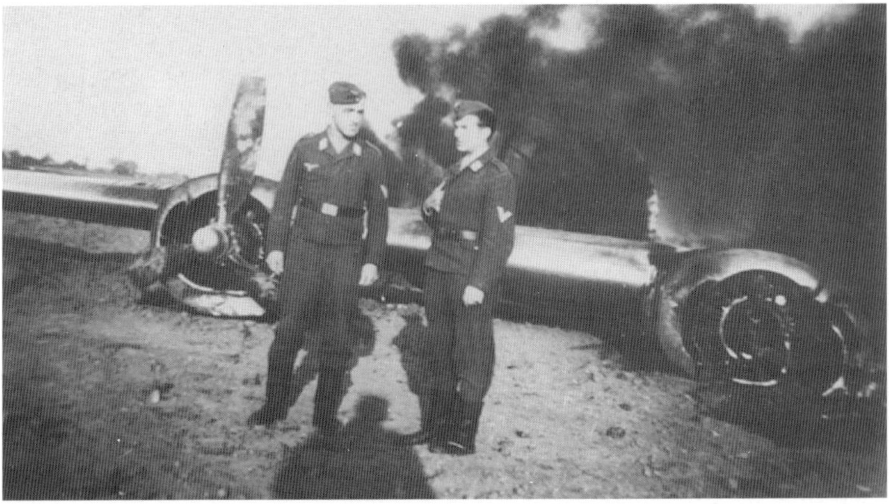

The wreckage of 'Boomerang' lies scattered and burning over Dutch soil.

Miraculously all but one of the crew walked away from this wreckage.

Other planes and crews of the 492$^{nd}$ were forced down in enemy territory. The Smith crew's B24 at Ghedi Airfield in Northern Italy. Two days later a P38 fighter was dispatched by the 8$^{th}$ Air Force to 'dispose' of the aircraft.

The Wesson crew who were damaged and on fire over Oberffaffenhofen on July 24$^{th}$ '44. They extinguished the fire in the bomb bay and then diverted their crippled B24 in to Dubendorf Airfield in Switzerland.
A/C 44-10496 Puritanical Bitch was only on her second mission with the 492$^{nd}$ Bomb Group. Such were the fortunes of war and the luck of the men of the 492$^{nd}$.

Despite these major setbacks, for the 492$^{nd}$ it was always back to work the next day…same routine, same bomb load, similar targets, the same dangers.

And the danger was there for the enemy as well, if this guy got you in the sights of his B24's waist gun, you were lucky if you got home that night.

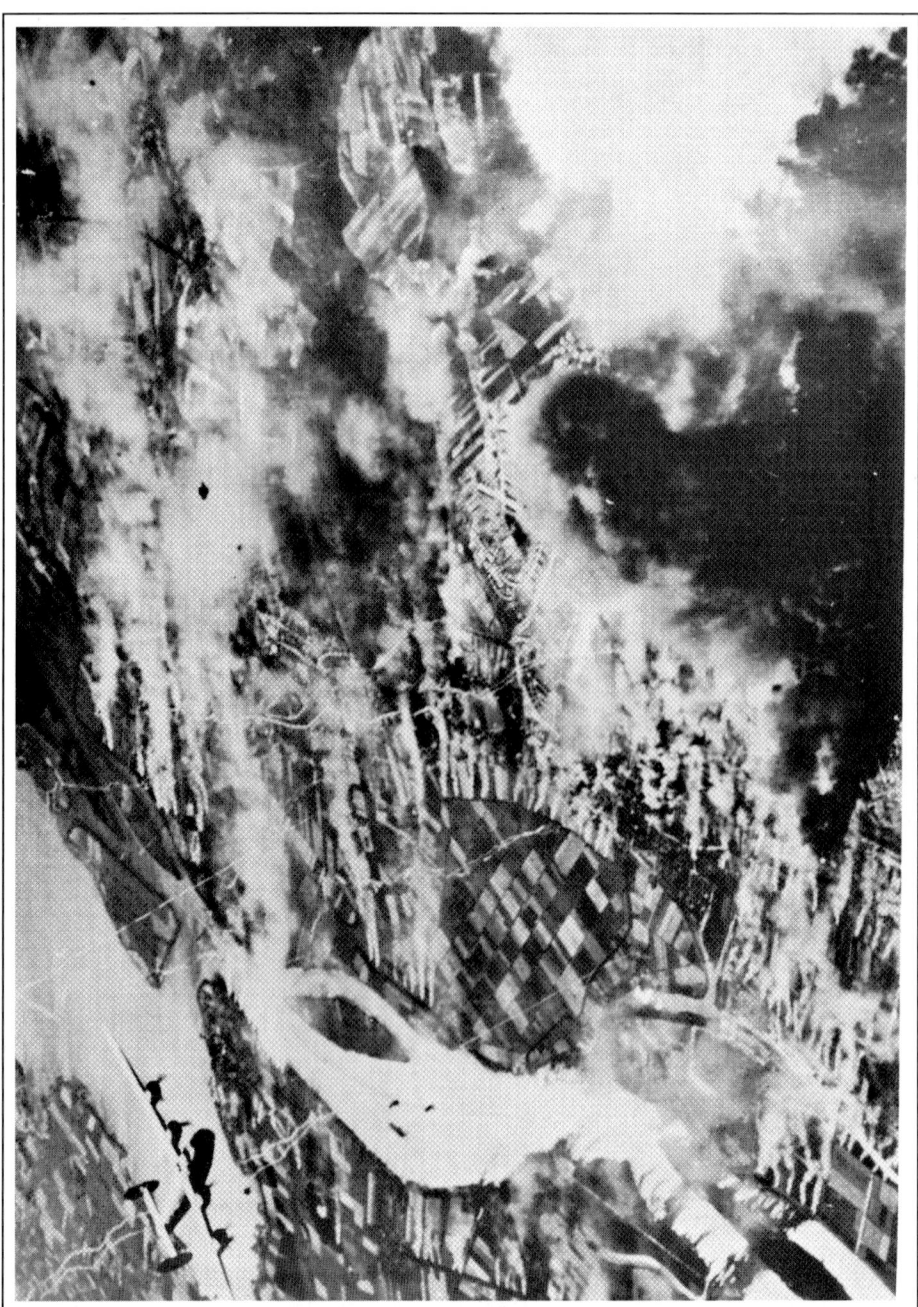

The main attack on June 20<sup>th</sup> 1944 was on the Baltic city of Politz, at the estuary of the river Oder. The 492<sup>nd</sup> had been there before and had taken a beating. Today it would be worse…much worse.

Kiel just over a month later…the 492$^{nd}$ fought on, bloodied but unbowed.

It was a pity you were either too busy or too scared to enjoy the view. Some days it could be really fabulous.
You wanted to fly with guys who were scared like you. If they weren't, they probably hadn't grasped the reality of what they were doing and where they were. That could be kinda worrying for the rest of the squadron.

Amazingly only one crewmember did not make it out of this carnage…

…and sadly only one survived from this. Tired crews and badly damaged planes could all conspire to make the mission end in disaster, even when you had made it back to your own airfield.

And this is what your airfield home looked like. A little basic, a little windswept and very khaki.

…nonetheless it was home, and it was where you and all your buddies lived.

And home was full of khaki huts. Some had round roofs and some had pointed roofs…
…however they were all khaki regardless of shape…

Generally you lived in the huts with the rounded roofs…

…and worked in the ones with the pointed roofs. Obviously the war budget didn't spread to lampshades!

It did not seem so long ago that the British flag was lowered and the Stars and Stripes raised…

…to many it seemed longer; but in a few short weeks a lot had happened to the men of the 492$^{nd}$.

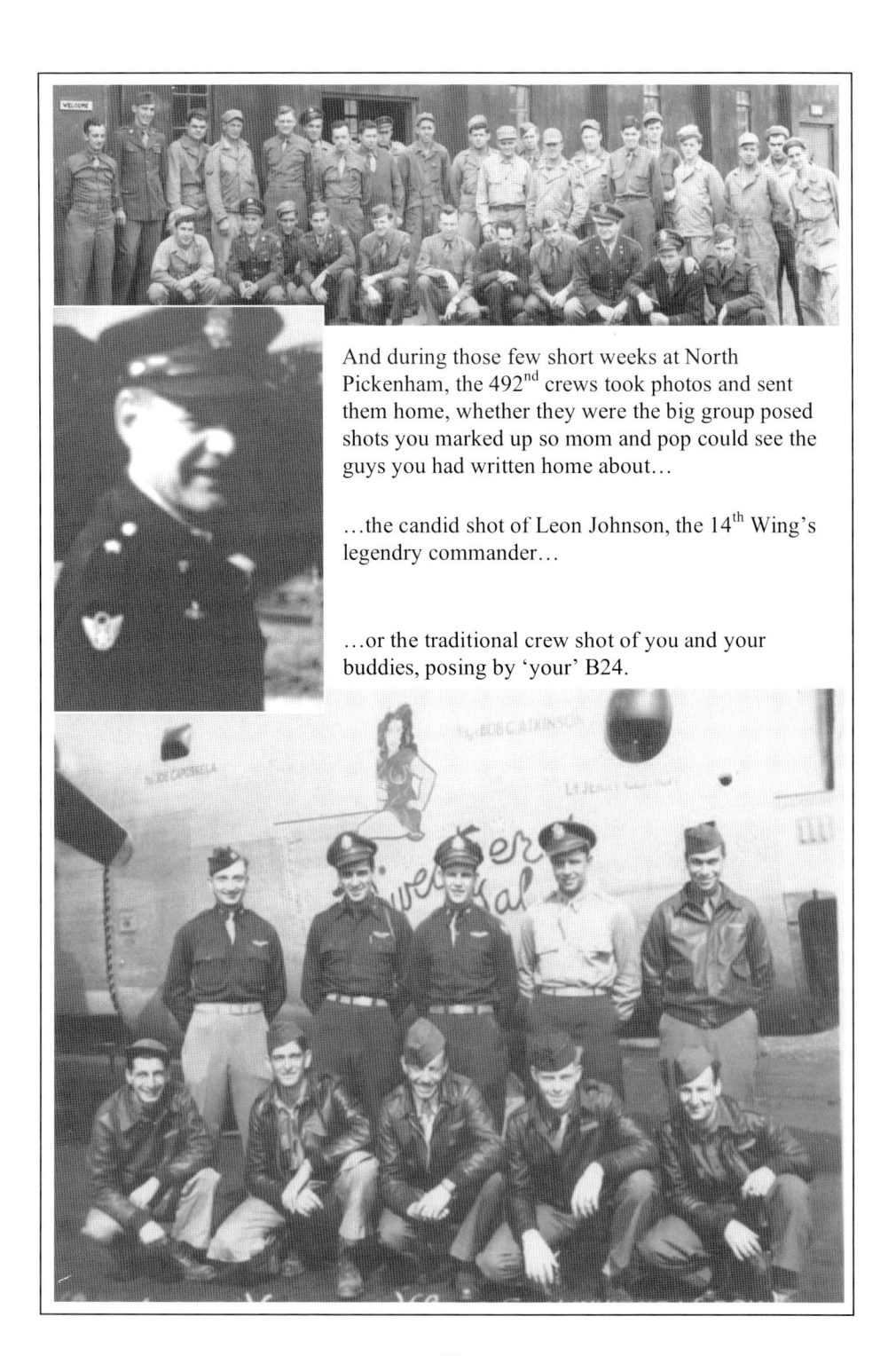

And during those few short weeks at North Pickenham, the 492$^{nd}$ crews took photos and sent them home, whether they were the big group posed shots you marked up so mom and pop could see the guys you had written home about…

…the candid shot of Leon Johnson, the 14$^{th}$ Wing's legendry commander…

…or the traditional crew shot of you and your buddies, posing by 'your' B24.

You and the boys posed together for your mission debrief…

…in front of the plane…

…or by the side of the plane. Either way it didn't matter; it was another photo to send home to the folks or to your girl, waiting for news thousands of miles away. Photos and letters to and from home were always a high priority.

Sadly they were sometimes the last ones your folks ever received.

The Herbert crew Lost 19th May 1944.

Sometimes a whole bunch of you could get together. But when you and your team were working round the clock, all day and every day, that could sometimes be a tall order.

For the ground crews of the 492$^{nd}$ this was the office,
Perched on a shiny B24 in the Norfolk countryside…

…overlooking the hut village that made up home.

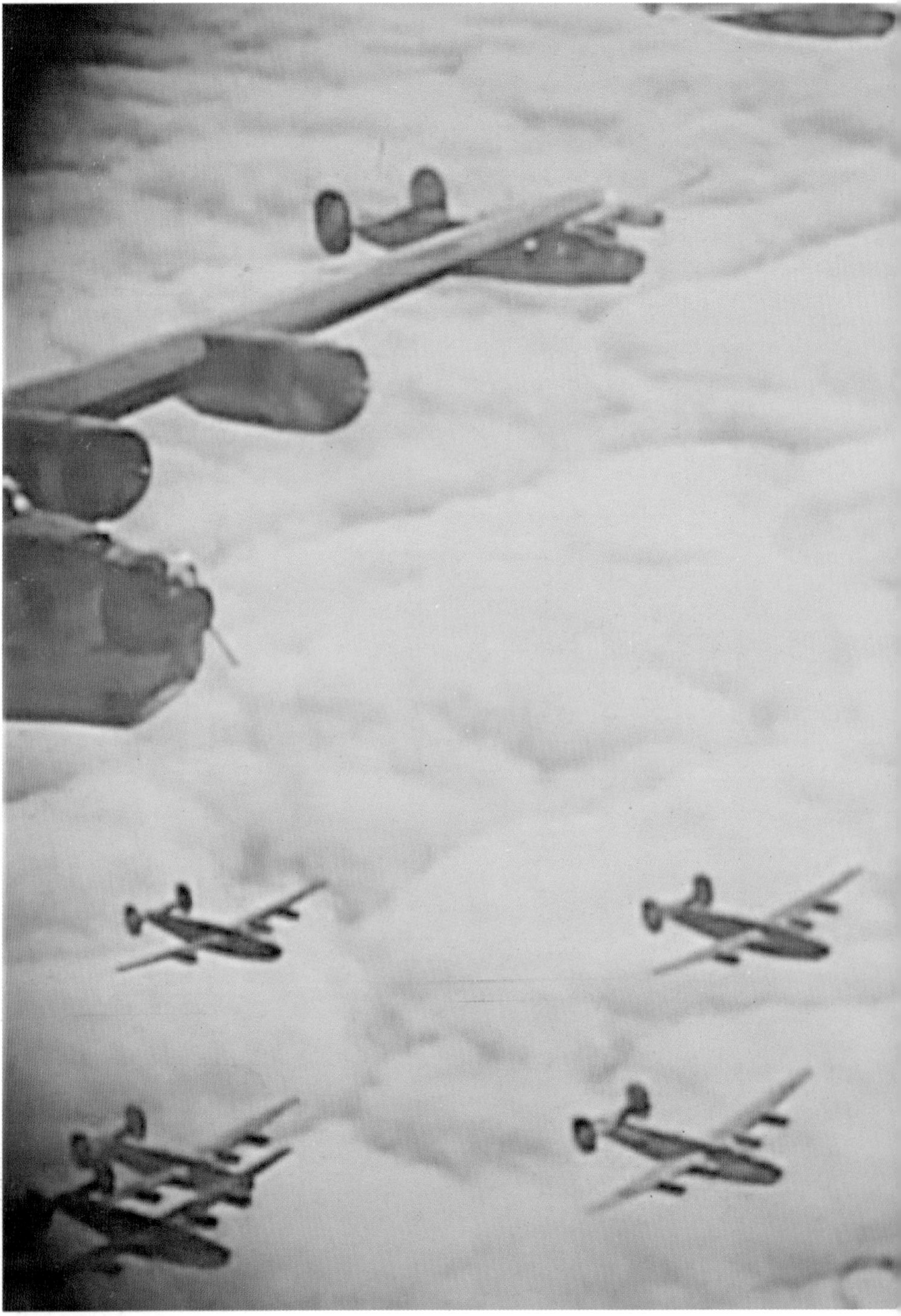

The B24s of the 492$^{nd}$ Bombard Group doing what they were good at, taking the fight to the enemy.

When you are flying this close to the plane beside you, you had better know what you are doing. These Liberators are probably doing 275 MPH or more and the planes are so close you could not get another one between them. When you remember there were often no auto pilots in use on these missions, that's precision flying at its best.

There was almost certainly a similar picture out of the right hand window and as part of the Second Air Division there was almost certainly another six or seven hundred planes in the same piece of sky at the same time. Added to this there were a load of allied fighter escorts and of course from time to time, a considerable number of German fighters all milling about determined to stop the B24s from doing their job.

The air over northern Europe got very busy on an almost daily basis.

Only very bad weather ever stopped them…and then not often.

Sometimes paperwork came on the large side…

…other times it was done for you, as this crew hopes as it heads to de-brief.

# The 491$^{St}$ Bombardment group.

The 491$^{St}$ Bombardment Group had been operating successfully for quite a while, from Station 366 (Metfield), in Suffolk; long before they moved to North Pickenham.
However one day in July1944, there was a devastating accident in the Metfield bomb dump. Sadly in the ensuing explosion, several airmen lost their lives and the collateral damage to the airfield infrastructure required that the 491$^{St}$ found a new home ...fast. North Pickenham would prove to be ideal.
On the 15th of August 1944, they re-located to Norfolk and continued their war with the Nazi regime.
Like the 492$^{nd}$ before them they were not handed an easy ride in the pursuit of victory and they were forced into a hard, blow for blow, grinding war, as the allied forces worked their way towards Berlin and final victory.

---

The demise of Metfield.
Captured from the same angle, but from different distances the mushroom cloud pinpoints the seat of the explosion, visible for many miles away.
The sound was however heard from a much greater distance, and reports at the time were received from over twenty-six miles away.
Little wonder that the 491$^{St}$ were in need of a new airfield.

The bomb dump was itself understandably a mess, but the damage to the remainder of the airfield was a real surprise when all the smoke had cleared and the dust had settled. Eleven B24s had either been destroyed or badly damaged.

Fortunately not all of the bombs had gone off.

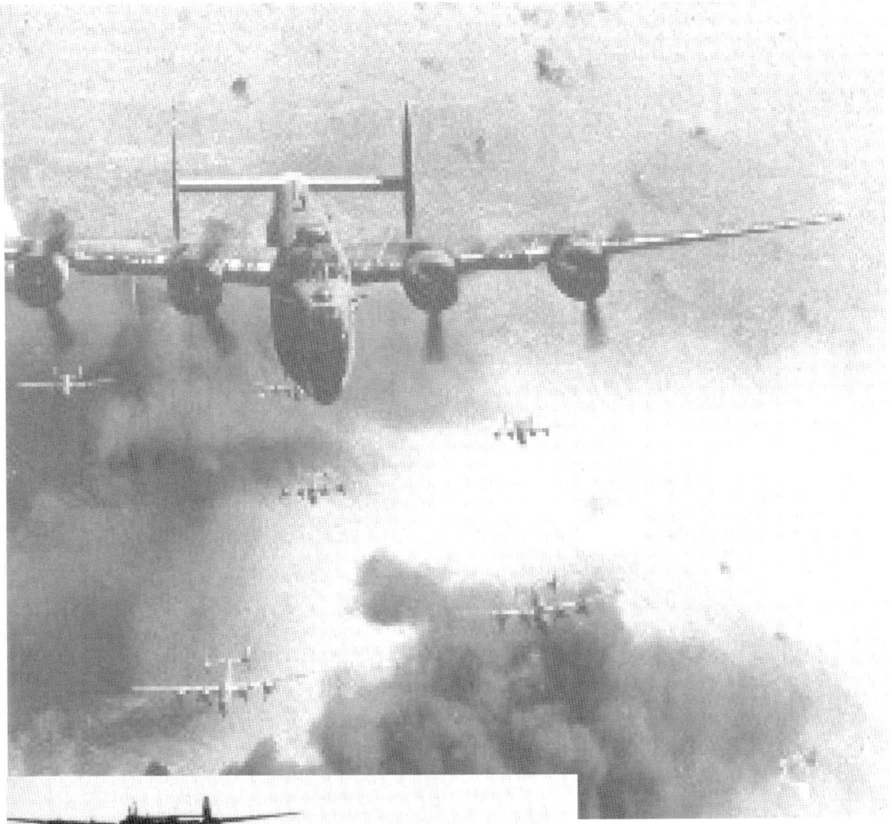

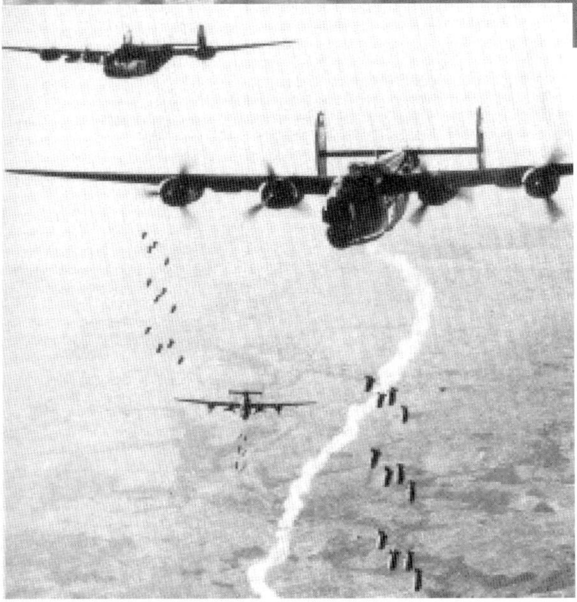

Just a few days after arriving at North Pickenham, it was the 491st that took off in the early morning and headed out in tight formation to further batter the Nazi industrial heartland.

Several hours later, the formation was still tight as they swept in and delivered their bomb load. Now all they had to do was get back to Norfolk. Not always as simple as it sounds…

...as the Hunter crew were to find out to their cost on a supply run to Holland. Sadly after executing a pretty good forced landing in a field near Eindhoven, Captain James Hunter's luck ran out. Off picture to the right (see inset) there was a collection of farm buildings and trees. Sadly there was only one survivor.

Even for the supply drop runs like the one to Eindhoven the crews practiced low level over their home airfield…

…then it was off to Holland to do it for real. With people starving to death, the crews knew it was as important as any bombing mission and no-one wanted to get it wrong.

Wham-Bam on an earlier raid on Hanover in late August with No1 engine on fire. Only two of the crew survived.

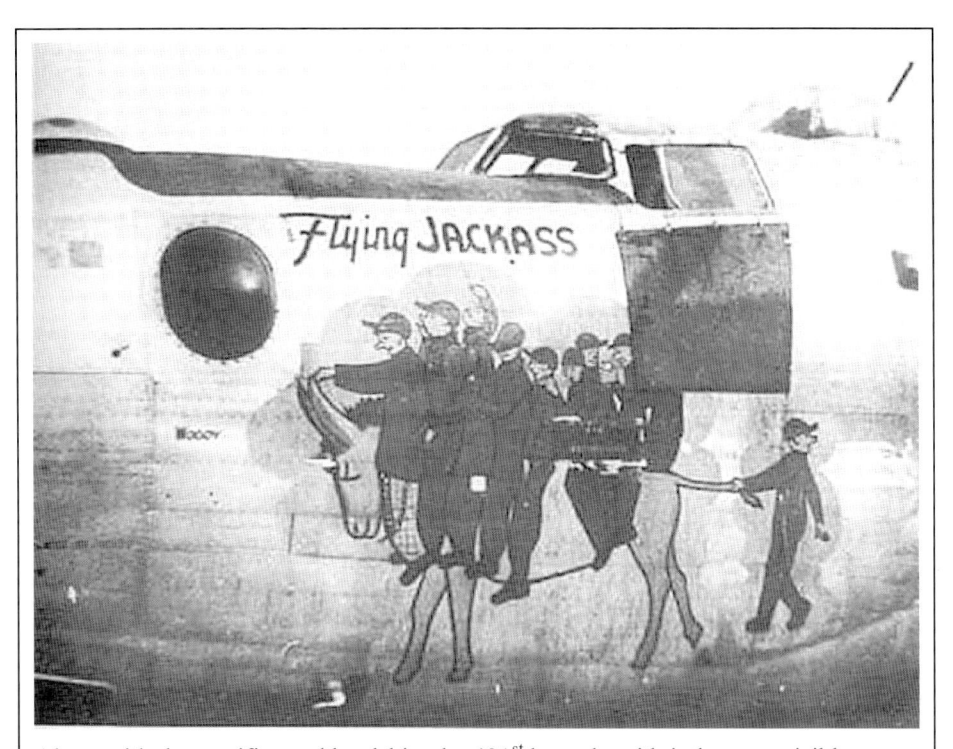

Along with the sacrifice and hardship, the 491$^{st}$ brought with it the very visible lighter side of the USAAF…Nose Art.

As tradition dictated in those days, glamour and humour shared the top billing.

Some were quite complex, carefully thought out and executed…

...to a level worthy of the film studios themselves.

Others were definitely produced to a hurried minimalist design, as the bombers were prepared for their main duty…

"MODEST MAIDEN—?"

Some were even obliterated in the course of that duty by your own team as well as the enemy. Maintenance crews had attached armour plate to Miss Francia …

… no doubt the boys who flew her were hoping the paint brushes would restore her to her full glory before too long.

She Devil at work, high above the cloud base…

…and at rest.

At work surrounded by other 491$^{st}$ BG bombers, heading southeast towards the target for today…

…some days you could avoid making con-trails, other days you couldn't.

Four to five hours after take off you could release your bomb load…

…any relief at making the target and doing your job accurately was wiped out when you saw your buddy's B24 spinning in over the target, with one wing already blown off by enemy action.

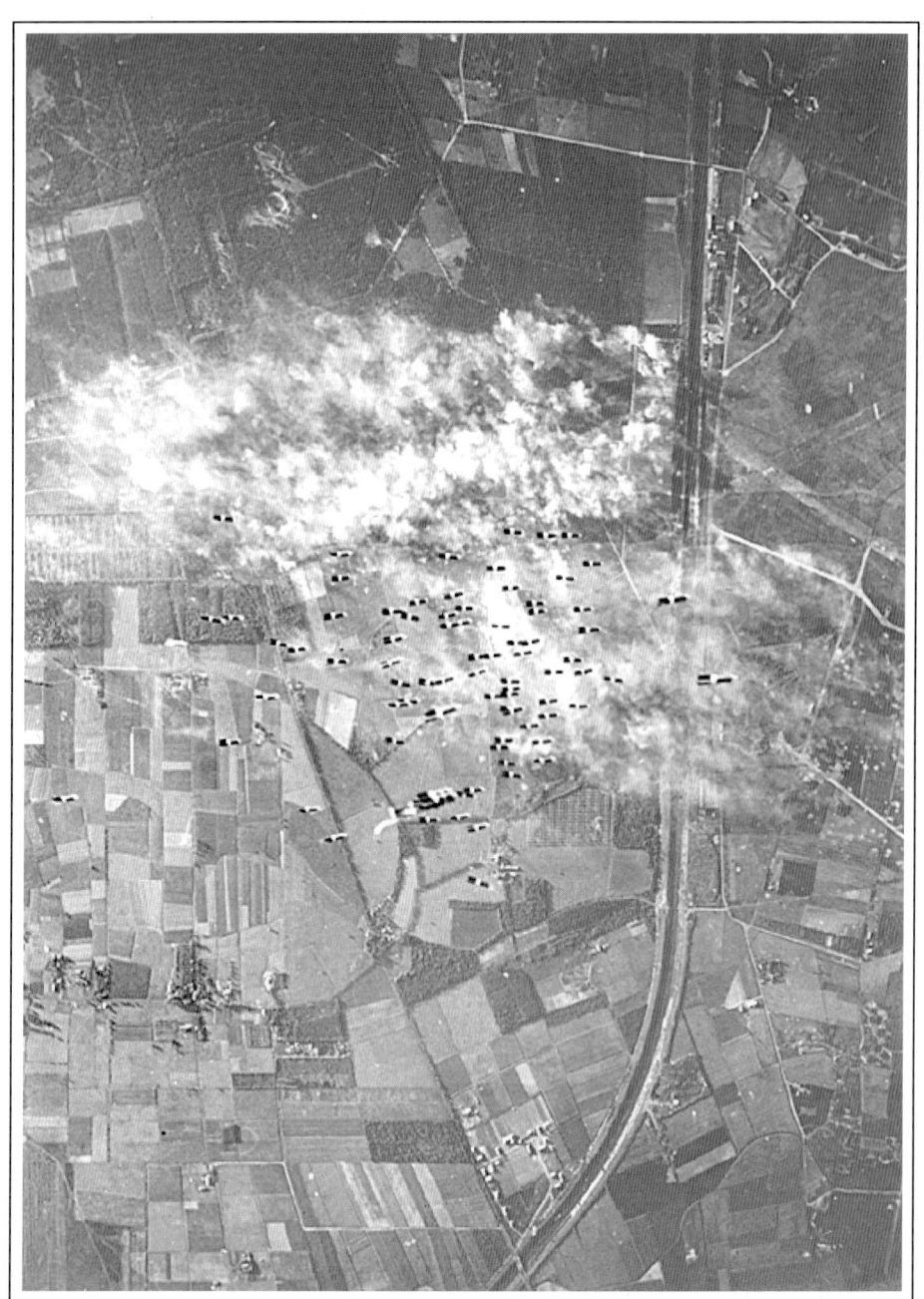

And this is what you came to do. Take out the enemy's ability to prolong the war. Road, rail and canal transport links were always a prime target as they slowed down supplies to the battle areas and caused additional burden on the enemy war machine.

Other missions were to support the ground troops as they fought their way towards Berlin. It was all in a days work to the 491st…

…whether the load was bombs or supplies, the B24s battled tirelessly to get them on target, on time.

The innocent looking little black puffs of smoke were flak...red hot lumps of sharp steel, travelling at very high speed…

…it could bring you down…

…it could kill and injure your crew...

…it could prevent you from completing your mission…

…above all else, it would always guarantee to get your attention.

But once you had got clear of it on the way home, the moment of touchdown was a feeling of real relief…

…you knew the flak had not got you…this time.

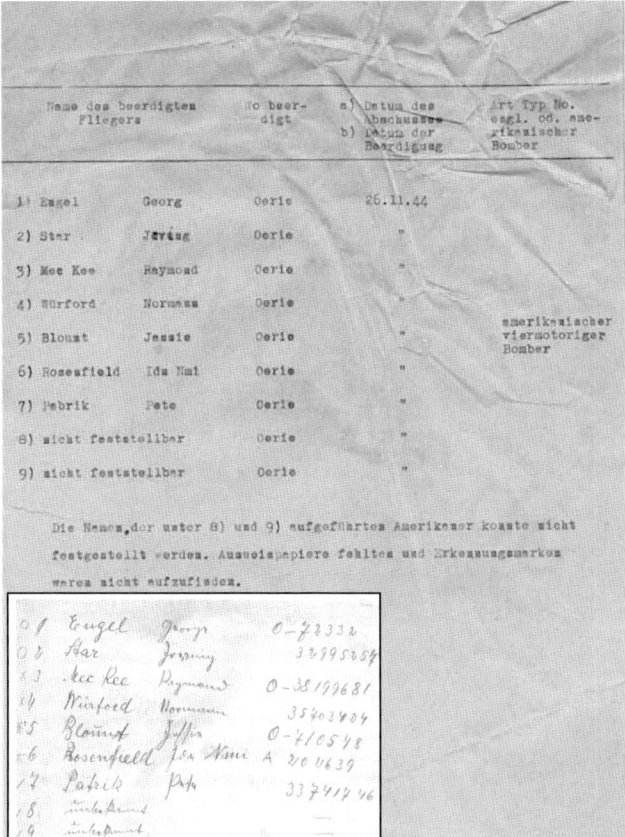

But it was fighters not flak that got Ark Angel, who met her fate near the small village of Oerie in the Hildesheim area of Germany, as part of an armada of planes tasked with bombing the synthetic oil plant at Hanover-Misburg.

Ark Angel, piloted by Lt David Bennett got into trouble following an attack by German Fighters and slowly drifted down and away from the formation. Lt Bennett eventually lost the battle to keep his crippled plane in the air as it neared Oerie. None of the crew survived.

This is the local and military paperwork recording the event.

Looking back in the formation it was good to see your buddies behind you. The good tight formation had worked as planned. It was however your tail gunner who got the best view.

Whether it was over the land, or the long expanses of sea you always had to cross twice on every mission, you always wanted to look out and see all four props on every plane in your group turning. Just three would do at this stage on the way home, as the planes were much lighter; any less and any crew, including your own, had a very few options left and only a slim chance of being home for supper that evening.

The chalk guide lines for the artist who painted Lucky Penny are still in place, so for sure it hadn't rained, or the plane been flown...
...so keen were the guys to have the shot taken, it wouldn't be surprising if the paint was still wet!

As much a tradition as nose art… the classic shot of you and your buddies in front of your B24 to send home to mom and pop was as mandatory as the mission briefing.

Although the posed crew photos were part of the ritual…

…sometimes the candid shots were far more telling. though they tended not to get sent home so often.

General Leon Johnson, the legendry commander of the 14$^{th}$ Combat Bombardment Wing (Heavy). Although based at Shipdham, Leon Johnson commanded the 14$^{th}$ Wing from the first flight of the 492$^{nd}$ Bomb Group to the last of the 491$^{st}$ Bomb Group. His leadership and drive were some of the main components of the mix that made the 14$^{th}$ Wing and the 2$^{nd}$ Air Division one of the most successful sections of the USAAF between 1942 and 1945.

Heading home…in the spring of 1945 that had very significant double meaning.

Assembly ships were a common sight at the start of any mission heading to Europe from Norfolk. This is Rage in Heaven, the 491$^{st}$'s highly visible version. The zebra stripes on the wings and tail are green.
Rage in Heaven had been retired from operations in 1944 and carried the letter WW after her serial number on her tail fin, indicating that she was War Weary.
She crashed in January 1945.

But then in early May it was all over.
Over a three day period it went from flying 1,000 bomber strategic raids, to as-and-when tactical missions. If the build up to becoming operational had seemed to take forever, then the transition to not flying combat missions was dramatically quick. For a lot of pilots the majority of their flying from now on would be carrying passengers on sightseeing 'Trolley Missions'.

When Ruthless Ruthie blew a tyre on take off on the 16$^{th}$ of April, it was the last 'incident' of the war involving a B24 of the 491$^{st}$. For once, everyone walked away from the crash, and some time later they all got to go home...

...Job done.

```
                    AWARDED THE BRONZE STAR
Seargent CLARENCE R WENSKOVITCH 13190253 Air Force, United States Army. For
heroic service in connection with military operations against the enemy from
14 March to 30 April. During the bulge in Belgium. When it seemed impossible
for his ship to get away from the ten enemy fighters that were attacking them.
Seargent Wenskovitch, Realizing the urgent necessity of accurate shooting, shot
down six enemy fighters himself. Seargent Wenskovitch, kept on firing his guns
untill he had no more ammunition left, and the guns were servicable no more.
While firing on the enemy fighters Seargent Wenskovitch was wounded in the left
leg. He was later taken to the base hospital and treated for his serious wound.
Seargent Wenskovitch Seargent Wenskovitch's keen sence of responsibility for
his ship and his ship mates enabled him to carry out Successfully a most
important mission involving the security of his ship and crew.
```

Acts of heroism were no rarity in the history of North Pickenham. This notification of the award for a Bronze Star went to the tail gunner of B24 'Tubaro' in the Moutner crew, Sgt Robert Wenskovich.

Despite serious leg wounds Wenskovich stayed at his post and scored six kills and exhausted his supply of ammunition in his successful efforts to ward off a swarm of German fighters and enable the rest of his crew to complete their bombing mission over Belgium.

> IN MEMORY TO
> THE MEN OF THE USAAF
> WHO FLEW FROM
> NORTH PICKENHAM
> 1944 – 1945
> 492 B.G.
> APRIL 1944 – AUGUST 1944
> 491 B.G.
> AUGUST 1944 – MAY 1945

Neither bomb group is ever forgotten by the people of Norfolk. This memorial is in the village of North Pickenham.

To find it, take the road from Swaffham to North Pickenham Village. Turn right just after the radio mast and simply follow the signs to the industrial estate, just inside the village boundary. The memorial stands on your right, regularly tended, at the entrance to a small housing complex.

**Cover Painting.**
The cover painting by Alex Jay depicts two B24s from North Pickenham, one from the 491$^{st}$ and the other from the 492$^{nd.}$ The one from the 492$^{nd}$ was flown by 2$^{nd}$ Lt Charles Arnett and the one from the 491$^{st}$ by Charles's best friend Captain Wayne Stewart.
Despite being shot down over Holland whilst on a bombing mission to Brunswick, on May 19$^{th}$ 1944, Charles Arnett survived the war. Sadly Wayne Stewart did not, his plane failing to return from its 30$^{th}$ and final mission. Any USAAF crew completing 30 missions could expect to go home once they had landed back at base.

The remains of Boomerang; 2$^{nd}$ Lt Charles Arnett's B24 burns in a field near Tuitenhorn in Holland. Minutes earlier the Arnett crew became POWs.

The author gratefully acknowledges assistance from many sources, especially the Arnett Historical Group, but claims all errors and omissions as his own.

**Cover painting**. Alex Jay. www.blueskygalleries.co.uk
**Photo acknowledgements:-**
The unique colour photos in the centre pages include frames captured from rare early colour footage taken from the Mahoney archive.

| | |
|---|---|
| The Arnett Historical Group | Brian Mahoney |
| Alan Sirrell | USAAF |
| Alan Blue/USAAF | Steve Adams |
| The Coulthart Collection | ©2006 The estate of the late James J. Mahoney |
| The Hunter Collection | The estate of the late Sgt R. Wenskovich |
| The Community of Oerie | |

For further study please go to:- www.492bg.com and www.491st.org

# Facts and Figures on the 492$^{nd}$ and 491$^{st}$

|  | **492nd** | **491st** |
|---|---|---|
| **Arrived** | 14$^{th}$ April 1944 | 15$^{th}$ August 1944 |
| **Departed** | 12$^{th}$ August 1944 | 4$^{th}$ July 1945 |
| **Aircraft Used** | Consolidated Liberator B24 | |
| | *4 x 1,200 Pratt & Witney Radial engines* | |
| | *10 man crew* | |
| | *Bomb load – 6 tons* | |
| | *All up weight – 29 tons* | |
| | *Top Speed – 290 MPH* | |
| | *Service Ceiling – 28,000 ft* | |
| | *Fuel Load – up to 3,516 gallons* | |
| | *Range – 2,100 miles* | |
| **Bomb Group** | *2$^{nd}$ Bombardment Wing (H)* | |
| **Complement** | *492$^{nd}$ Bombardment Group Headquarters 491$^{st}$* | |
| | *856$^{th}$ Bombardment Squadron (H)* | *852$^{nd}$* |
| | *857$^{th}$ Bombardment Squadron (H)* | *853$^{rd}$* |
| | *858$^{th}$ Bombardment Squadron (H)* | *854$^{th}$* |
| | *859$^{th}$ Bombardment Squadron (H)* | *855$^{th}$* |
| | *479$^{th}$ Sub Depot* | *476$^{th}$* |
| | *1450$^{th}$ Ordnance Company* | *1802$^{nd}$* |
| | *882$^{nd}$ Chemical Company (AD)* | *807$^{th}$* |
| | *1261$^{st}$ Military Police Company* | *983$^{rd}$* |
| | *2108$^{th}$ Engineer Fire Fighting Platoon* | *2108$^{th}$* |
| | *1234$^{th}$ Quartermaster Company* | *1230$^{th}$* |
| | *2967$^{th}$ Finance Company* | *208$^{th}$* |
| | *266$^{th}$ Medical Company* | *266$^{th}$* |
| **Missions** | 66 (Sorties 1602) | (5005 Sorties) 187 |
| **Ordnance dropped** | 3,643   *Tons* | 12,304 |
| **Losses 1944-1945** | 55      *Planes* | 70 |
| | 530     *Men* | 700 |
| | | *(includes Metfield data)* |